Workbook

For

James Clear's

Atomic Habits

The Step by Step Guide To Turn Your Goals Into Reality

Companion Works

Table of Contents

How To Use This Workbook...1

Introduction...4

PART ONE: THE FUNDAMENTALS: WHY TINY
CHANGES MAKE A BIG DIFFERENCE.....................7

Ch 1: The Surprising Power of Atomic Habits.............7

Ch 2: How Your Habits Shape Your Identity (and Vice
Versa)...15

Ch 3: How to Build Better Habits in 4 Simple Steps .24

PART TWO: THE 1ST LAW: MAKE IT OBVIOUS.......33

Ch 4: The Man Who Didn't Look Right 33

Ch 5: The Best Way to Start a New Habit 38

Ch 6: Motivation is Overrated; Environment Often
Matters More 43

Ch 7: The Secret of Self-Control 47

PART THREE: THE 2ND LAW: MAKE IT
ATTRACTIVE 51

Ch 8: How to Make a Habit Irresistible...................51

Ch 9: The Role of Family and Friends in Shaping Your
Habits..57

Ch 10: How to Find and Fix the Causes of Your Bad
Habits..62

PART FOUR: THE 3RD LAW: MAKE IT EASY........... 67

Ch 11: Walk Slowly, but Never Backward 67

Ch 12: The Law of Least Effort................................. 70

Ch 13: How to Stop Procrastinating by Using the Two-Minute Rule.. 74

Ch 14: How to Make Good Habits Inevitable and Bad Habits Impossible... 79

PART FIVE: THE 4TH LAW: MAKE IT SATISFYING.. 83

Ch 15: The Cardinal Rule of Behavior Change 83

Ch 16: How to Stick with Good Habits Every Day..... 88

Ch 17: How an Accountability Partner Can Change Everything... 93

PART SIX: ADVANCED TACTICS HOW TO GO FROM BEING MERELY GOOD TO BEING TRULY GREAT... 96

Ch 18: The Truth About Talent (When Genes Matter and When They Don't) 96

Ch 19: The Goldilocks Rule; How to Stay Motivated in Life and Work 101

Ch 20: The Downside of Creating Good Habits....... 105

Conclusion: The Secret to Results That Last 109

Little Lessons from the Four Laws 110

How To Use This Workbook

Hello there!

It is a great pleasure to see that you have taken an interest in the book "Atomic Habits" by James Clear. This book by James is arguably one of the best in terms of self-development and habit formation. Filled with workable strategies and simple to follow ideas, you will find picking up good habits and kicking away bad ones to be such a breeze!

This workbook is meant to enhance and highlight the ideas and concepts mentioned, so that it makes it very much easier for you to take action and implement what you have learnt from the book into practical, daily usage. With the aid of this workbook, taking that step forward to becoming a better, more productive you is very much easier. You will be guided step by step to become familiar with the methods James teaches in Atomic Habits. In order to learn quicker and with a lasting impact, it is vital that you answer all the questions presented in the workbook, and answer them sincerely. Only by digging deep and giving honest answers will you be able to flash light on what truly matters to you, and get the opportunities to effect lasting positive change in your daily life.

The workbook will also feature important summaries of each individual chapter, which will be integral in helping you answer the questions contained therein. As such, for the time constrained folk, you do not necessarily need to read the main book before answering the questions in this workbook. All the crucial points have been condensed and captured for your attention. For the folks whom have already read the book, the afore mentioned salient concepts will serve well as quick reminders and gentle nudges when you are doing the questions.

Whilst attempting the questions found in the workbook, please take your time to go through it carefully. This portion is an area where speedy reading can be set aside and replaced with thoughtful ruminations. The questions will encourage you to reflect and think, sometimes very deeply, before you jump in with any answers. It will be of great benefit to you if the answers supplied are colored with the honesty of thought and tinged with sincerity. After all, no one can be as interested in your welfare as your own self.

Done in this careful, constructive way, you will be able to harness the positive change created and see it reverberate throughout many aspects of your life. For some, the honest answers may create self criticism. Take heart, know that you are not alone, and that by just the mere act of acknowledgement of mistakes made in the past, that itself is a very important step forward.

You will want to come back to these questions again after your initial foray, say after a period of 4 to 8 weeks; there really is no set in stone time length, but it is highly recommended to have at least a space of 4 weeks between the first and second attempt at the questions. This second try is really to let you see the progress you have made, both in thoughts and actions, and also to think of different angles to the same questions with your new life experiences.

You can really repeat this process as many times as you find useful. The key is always honesty in the answers and an indefatigable spirit for self development and progress.

May you be well and be happy.

Introduction

James Clear, the author of Atomic Habits, was accidentally hit in the face with a baseball bat when he was in his sophomore year in high school. The accident left him in a bad state that he had to be flown to a bigger hospital in Cincinnati, where James had to be "put into a medically induced coma." When he was released from the hospital, he had a bulging left eye, a broken nose, and about half a dozen facial fractures.

Back home, James had to undergo physical therapy. It took him eight months before he could drive again and one year to go back to baseball. However, it was not an easy return to the thing James loved the most. He was removed from the varsity baseball team, and it saddened him. Even when James managed to make it to the varsity team as a senior a year later, his baseball record was not something to be proud of. James knew that he had to make things happen for him if he wanted to improve his game.

His opportunity came when James went to college at Denison University, two years after his accident. He was happy for making it as a college athlete, although he was at the bottom of the roster. James began to develop good habits that eventually brought back his self-confidence. His academic and athletic achievements reflected the effect of the habits James developed. When he graduated, James was awarded the President's Medal, the university's highest academic honor.

Although James became the university's top male athlete and made it to the ESPN Academic All America Team, he never became a professional player. But he was proud for having fulfilled his potential despite his injury.

James realized that small changes which may seem trivial would build into something amazing if we make it a habit. The more we improve on our habits, the better the quality of our lives become. His passage from being broken to achieving accomplishments was a never ending progress that started with baby steps, and James was happy that these steps brought him to where he is right now.

He documented his experiences as he developed his habits, and in November 2012, he decided to share these experiences. He began the habit of publishing a new article every Monday and Friday, and after a year of doing that, he had over thirty thousand email subscribers. The subscriptions continued to grow tremendously, making James to have one of the fastest-growing online newsletters.

In 2015, Penguin Random House commissioned James to write this book–by then, he was known as an expert on habits. James also became a resource person for behavior change, habit formation, and continuous improvement for top companies. A year later, major publications such as Entrepreneur, Forbes, and Time began to feature his articles.

James launched the Habit Academy in 2017. The Academy became the leading training platform for those who wanted to build better work and personal habits. Sometime in 2018, as he was about to finish his Atomic Habits book, his newsletter via jamesclear.com had almost half a million subscribers.

Through this book, James shares a practical guide for building habits that will stick for life. The book is a blend of ideas drawn from James' experiences and significant scientific discoveries relevant to habit formation.

PART ONE:
THE FUNDAMENTALS: WHY TINY CHANGES MAKE A BIG DIFFERENCE

Ch 1: The Surprising Power of Atomic Habits

Summary

For almost one century, British professional cyclists agonized over mediocrity, winning only one gold medal in the Olympics and not a single victory in the Tour de France. Their performance was so dismal that one of Europe's top bike manufacturers refused to sell to the team.

In 2003, the governing body for Great Britain's professional cycling called British Cycling hired Dave Brailsford to be its performance director. He led the team with the principle of breaking down everything that goes into cycling and making a small improvement in each, then putting them together to achieve significant progress.

Brailsford and the team's coaches made small changes, ranging from redesigning bike seats to improving the bike tire's grip, the material of their bike wear, and hiring a surgeon who trained cyclists on proper handwashing to avoid catching a cold.

From 2007 to 2017, British cyclists conquered the world of cycling as they brought home sixty-six Olympic or Paralympic gold medals, 178 world championships, and five Tour de France wins.

What spelled the difference? Brailsford targeted multiple, small, but useful improvements.

We tend to associate huge success with mammoth actions, not realizing that small improvements are more meaningful. A little act may not be substantial at first glance, but its effects will multiply as we repeat it over time.

If we improve 1% daily for one year, we end up 37% better at the end of the year. If we decline by 1% daily for one year, we go downhill. However, most of us want quick results, so that if we do not see a significant improvement in ourselves, we go back to our previous routines. A small change in our daily habits can determine who we could become.

Right now, you might be far from your goal, but with the right habits, you can achieve the success you want. On the other hand, you might be experiencing success now; however, your bad habits might lead you to fail if you do not correct those habits eventually.

Habits can work both ways–they can lead to your success or your failure. You must understand how it works and how it affects you.

Productivity, knowledge, and relationships build up. Completing an additional task every day does not only give you a sense of accomplishment; it enables you to master new skills, allowing your brain to focus on other areas that you can develop. Learning one new thing each day opens your mind to new ideas and ways of thinking. The more we interact well with other people, the stronger our connection with them becomes; the stronger our connection, the broader our network gets.

However, stress, negative thoughts, and outrage can also intensify if left unchecked. Typical stress such as dealing with financial obligations should be manageable, but it can compound into serious health issues if it continues on for years. When you develop the habit of seeing the ugly in yourself and situations, you begin to paint all other people and situations as negative. Gripes, uprisings, and protests result from daily frustrations and provocations that build up over time.

Building a lasting habit is a challenge. We make slight changes in our habits, but we do not immediately notice the result. This stage is called Valley of Disappointment. The temptation to give up becomes strong at this stage, but we must understand that habits should stick long enough to cross the Plateau of Latent Potential – the stage where your slow but steady progress results in a momentous achievement.

Crossing the Plateau of Latent Potential requires patience. It begins with a single decision to change, which, when done repeatedly, grows into a habit.

Time and again, we have been taught that we can succeed if we have specific, workable goals. But the system or the process turns out to be more important than the goals. A goal gives you direction, but no matter how impressive your goal is, you are still likely to fail if you do not apply the appropriate process. But if you focus on what you need to do and what you need to improve on in order to progress, you will still achieve your goal.

Four problems can potentially arise if you focus too much on goals.

One: Winners and losers share the same goal.

The British cyclists aimed to win the Tour de France every year just like all other cyclists. They had the same goal but used different approaches to winning. It was not until the British cyclists introduced continuous improvements in their system that they started to win.

Two: Goal achievement is only temporary.

When your goal is to have a clutter-free workspace, you can organize and tidy up your workspace then you are happy that your workspace is clean. But when you keep at your habit of stacking up an assortment of documents and files on your table and not replacing things where they should be, your workspace becomes cluttered anew. You need to address your system, not your goals.

Three: A goal limits your happiness.

Some people hinge their success and happiness on achieving their goals, forgetting that there are various ways you can succeed and feel happy. The journey itself of pursuing your dream can be a source of joy, even if the result is not exactly how you envisioned it.

Four: A goal does not support long-term progress.

When a person achieves their goal, they tend to drop the habit they developed because they lose the motivation to practice it. A systems-focused mentality does not attach the habit to a single goal; it becomes a commitment to continuous improvement.

Habits may be likened to atoms – they are small, but their impact on our lives is powerful. Atomic habits are small actions that are easy to do but builds up over time to become a dominant force in our growth.

Lessons

1. Getting 1% better every day leads to a habit that compounds our actions' positive effects on our self.

2. Habits can work for or against us, so we need to understand the effect of our habits on us.

3. It takes time to reap the fruits of our small actions. We need to be patient and stick to our habits.

4. Atomic habits are anchored on small changes that lead to incredible results over time.

5. A systems-focused mindset brings better results than a goal-focused one.

Issues Surrounding the Subject Matter

1. Why is it more difficult to form good habits than break bad habits?

2. Why is it not ideal to make dramatic changes to achieve significant success?

3. What challenges have you experienced while building a habit?

4. How can you identify the habits which you want and those which you do not want?

5. Think back on a time where you had to labor hard without any result in sight, yet when you finally reached your goal, how did you feel? Correlate this to the plateau of latent potential.

Goals

1. How can you overcome the challenges of habit formation?

2. Reflect on where are the areas in your life which can benefit from positive habits and the kicking away of bad ones.

Action Steps

1. Think of a habit that you find difficult to develop. List down the challenges that you experienced or are currently experiencing while developing it.

2. Break down the habit into small components. For example, if you wish to develop healthy eating habits, you may want to consider how frequently you eat in a day, who eats with you, where you eat, who cooks the food for you, what kind of food you enjoy eating, etc.

3. For each component, identify small changes you need to make to ensure success. Decide which of these are easily doable.

4. Monitor your progress.

Checklist

1. Look for people who succeeded in developing the same habit. Start with your network of family, friends, co-workers, etc., and learn from their experience.

2. You may come up with a long list of what needs to be done or changed. Limit your list to those which are manageable. For each item on your list, identify what will make it work. For example, if you see the need to come up with a weekly menu, you might need a list of healthy dishes with their corresponding recipes.

Ch 2: How Your Habits Shape Your Identity (and Vice Versa)

Summary

As you form your habits, you will discover that it is easy to keep bad habits than building the good ones, regardless of your motivation. One reason is this: we are trying to change the wrong things.

There are three levels at which change can happen:

1. Outcomes. This level is about changing the consequences of your action. You focus on what you want to achieve, e.g., your goals. It is concerned about what you get in the end. A lot of people would opt to begin their change at this level.

2. Processes. The change at this level is centered on your habits and systems. It pertains to what you do.

3. Identity. This level is the deepest layer, where you change your beliefs about yourself and others. You can start your change at this level, as you establish who you wish to become.

All levels are useful, with none better than the others. However, a lot of people are most likely to begin their change at the outcome level. For example, you refuse a cigarette because you want to quit smoking.

Beginning with the identity level is more effective. When you resist e a cigarette because you are not a smoker, you are acting based on your belief that smoking is no longer a part of your current life. Unfortunately, most people leave out identity change in their self-image equation. They set goals and plan to achieve them, but they never consider how they see themselves.

Our beliefs drive our actions; our habits are developed based on the identity we want. If we want to improve ourselves, we also need to change who we are. We become more motivated to stick to our habits linked with the aspect of our identity that we are proud of. For example, if you are proud of your knitting skills, you will be more inclined to knit regularly.

Your motivation triggers the habit, but it is your identity that makes the habit stick. Your actions become natural when they are associated with the person you believe you are. However, identity change is a double-edged sword. It can work for you and become your strong ally for self-improvement, but it can also work against you when you fail to let go of your negative beliefs and accept these beliefs as facts about yourself.

The more strongly attached your actions are to your identity, the more difficult it is to change them. We tend to hold on to a group identity based on culture and personal identity that we maintain even if they do not reflect our true self. This inclination, referred to as identity conflict, poses an obstacle to positive change. You may come up with many excuses as to why you cannot stick to your habit, but what all this boils down to is your self-image. You would most probably need to unlearn some of your beliefs.

Your beliefs are acquired from your collection of experiences, which serve as proofs of your identity. Going to the gym regularly regardless of the weather condition is evidence that you are fitness conscious. The more evidence you have, the more intense your beliefs become and the clearer your self-image is.

Your habits personify your identity. Although your habits are not the only factors that establish your identity, it becomes the most important one because of the frequency with which your actions are repeated.

Each action that you take contributes to the person you wish to become. Each small habit that you develop provides evidence of a new identity. Changing your identity means willfully changing what you do.

Every habit that you develop teaches you to trust yourself as you accomplish new things. However, you will be forming bad habits as well, and those will also affect your identity. But that is okay. No one is perfect. The challenge is for you to develop more good habits than bad.

Identity change requires two major steps:

1. Decide who you want to be. If you do not know where to begin, start with your goal. Determine what kind of person will deliver the result you want to achieve. For example, if your goal is to lose weight, you may ask yourself, "Who is that kind of person who can lose 50 pounds?" The answers you provide can shift your focus from outcome to identity and can lead to a new set of beliefs, e.g., "I am the kind of person who has the discipline to observe my diet and exercise regularly."

2. Gather pieces of evidence to bolster the identity. When you know who you want to become, you can start taking baby steps to change your identity. Always use your desired identity as your compass. Following the example above, you can ask yourself, "What would a disciplined person eat for dessert – a small slice of chocolate cake or a selection of fresh fruits?"

The relationship between identity and habits is two-way. Your habits form your identity just as your identity forms your habits, creating a loop. Shaping your identity is a dynamic process. Choose who you want to become and choose the habits to reinforce your identity.

Lessons

1. Change happens at three levels: outcome, process, and identity.

2. It is more effective to apply identity-based instead of outcome-based changes to form a habit.

3. Your identity is not a constant. You must continuously upgrade and expand it.

4. Habits shape your identity, and your identity develops your habits, forming a habit loop.

Issues Surrounding the Subject Matter

1. Do you have negative beliefs about yourself? What are these beliefs, and how have these affected your habit formation?

2. What is the problem with developing outcome-based instead of identity-based changes?

3. Think back to instances where you thought you had formed positive habits, only to let them go after a while. Reflect back on what could have been done to properly maintain them and keep them as part of your life.

4. Get some quiet time and create a mental picture of who you desire to be. Bear in mind this positive tinkering should also be taken in a step by step approach. Use that positive mental self image and link it to good habits which you want to form and bad habits which you want to kick.

Goals

1. How do you intend to change your negative beliefs about yourself?
2. Think of 3 practical ways which you can do in order to maintain your habits

Action Steps

1. Describe the person you are now. Write down your descriptions, so you do not miss anything. Categorize your descriptions into positive beliefs and negative beliefs.

2. Evaluate each negative belief. Cross out those based on how other people perceive you but you do not believe to be true. Ensure that the entries you cross out are still readable.

3. Describe the person you want to become. Fill in only the portion on positive beliefs.

4. Identify habits you need to form and those you need to break to develop your desired identity.

5. Select one habit that you would like to form. Prioritize.

Checklist

1. Use the sample format below to write down your descriptions. Be specific

2. Compare your entries in the two columns. Under "Who I Want to Become," mark all entries that are not found in the "Who I Am Today" column.

3. Refer to all marked entries in the "Who I Want to Become" and all remaining entries in the Negative Beliefs cells to identify habits you want to form and those you need to break.

4. Consistent with the concept of 1% improvement, prioritize a habit that will not take much effort but you think will create the greatest impact.

	WHO I AM TODAY	WHO I WANT TO BECOME
Positive Beliefs		
Negative Beliefs		

	WHO I AM TODAY	WHO I WANT TO BECOME
Positive Beliefs		
Negative Beliefs		

Ch 3: How to Build Better Habits in 4 Simple Steps

Summary

In 1898, psychologist Edward Thorndike experimented with cats to understand how habits are formed. The experiment revealed that behaviors causing rewarding outcomes tend to be repeated, while those that yield unpleasant outcomes are more likely to be avoided.

A habit is a frequently repeated behavior that becomes automatic; it is formed through trial and error.

When you experience something new, your brain decides on how to respond to the situation. Your brain processes and analyzes new information, conceives options, and chooses the most viable action. When you choose an action that makes you feel rewarded, your brain registers that action.

This sums up the feedback loop that drives human behavior: try, fail, learn, try a new approach. Eventually, your brain picks up the practical actions and reinforces them, forming into a habit. When you face the same problem repeatedly, your brain automatically feeds you that action.

When you create habits, the activity in your brain decreases because it no longer analyzes the situation and omits the trial-and-error process. You know already what to look for and what to do given the same situation. Your brain creates an "if-then" rule.

Habits do not confine you to dull, boring routines; it liberates you from them. Habits create a mental space that allows you to think freely and creatively. They enable you to face new challenges and learn from them.

There are four steps of habit formation:

1. Cue

The cue triggers our brain to start a behavior. Your mind is continually looking for internal and external sources of rewards; the cue predicts a reward.

2. Cravings

Cravings motivate a habit. You do not crave for the habit itself, but you crave the change you experience when you form a habit. When you do not crave a change, you will not see the need to develop a habit. For example, you do not crave watching TV for the sake of looking at the television itself, but you desire to be entertained by what you see on screen.

Cravings are subjective, which means that given the same cue, two people may react differently. For example, a pair of leather shoes on sale may be a compelling trigger for someone who is often in a suit or corporate attire but will not attract a track and field athlete.

3. Response

This step refers to the habit you perform. It depends on your level of motivation, the amount of effort you are willing to apply, and your ability to execute the action.

4. Reward

A reward has a two-pronged purpose. The first is to satisfy your craving, and the second is to teach us which actions are helpful and worth remembering.

The cue recognizes the reward, the craving makes you want the reward, and the response helps you obtain the reward, which is the end goal of every habit.

The first three steps deliver the behavior; the reward encourages repeated demonstration of the behavior. If any of these steps are missing or lacking, you will not form a habit.

The four steps form an infinite cycle known as the habit loop. This loop can be divided into two phases. The first phase is the problem phase, comprised of cue and cravings. You realize the need to change at this phase. The second phase is the solution phase, which is composed of response and reward. This phase is where you act and achieve your desired change.

These four steps translate into a simple framework of developing good habits and eliminating bad ones. James refers to this as the Four Laws of Behavior Change.

The four rules are as follows:

Rule	To Form a Good Habit	To Break a Bad Habit	Relevant Step
1st	Make it obvious	Make it invisible	Cue
2nd	Make it attractive	Make it unattractive	Cravings
3rd	Make it easy	Make it difficult	Response
4th	Make it satisfying	Make it unsatisfying	Reward

Lessons

1. A habit is behavior repeated often to become automatic.

2. Habits aim to solve life problems with as little energy as possible.

3. The habit loop has four steps: cue, cravings, response, and reward.

4. There are Four Laws of Behavior Change you can apply in improving habits: (a) Make it obvious, (b) Make it attractive, (c) Make it easy, and (d) Make it satisfying.

Issues Surrounding the Subject Matter

1. What potential problems are there when:

    a. The cue is not apparent?

    b. The craving is not strong enough?

    c. Can you not respond to a craving as you wish?

    d. The reward is not clear to you?

2. Have you had a habit you wanted to form but failed? What obstacles did you encounter?

Goals

1. Using your worksheet from Chapter 2, what habit will you develop to build your desired identity? How do you intend to develop this habit?

Action Steps

1. Identify the habit you would like to build.
2. Examine the habit using the 4-step framework of habit formation. List as many cues you can think of.

Checklist

1. Refer to your Chapter 2 activity. You have identified the habit you like to prioritize, but you might want to review the need to replace it with another habit.

2. Use the worksheet format below to explore the 4-step framework for behavioral change.

Habit			
Cue	Craving	Response	Reward or Punishment

Habit			
Cue	Craving	Response	Reward or Punishment

Habit			
Cue	Craving	Response	Reward or Punishment

Habit			
Cue	Craving	Response	Reward or Punishment

Habit			
Cue	Craving	Response	Reward or Punishment

Habit			
Cue	Craving	Response	Reward or Punishment

Habit			
Cue	Craving	Response	Reward or Punishment

PART TWO:
THE 1ST LAW: MAKE IT OBVIOUS

Ch 4: The Man Who Didn't Look Right

Summary

A paramedic who has worked for several years with heart failure can immediately recognize if something is wrong with a person. A military analyst can identify an enemy missile despite the absence of a distinguishing sign.

The human brain compiles and sorts all information it discovers. When an experience is repeated, your brain picks up the lessons learned from it, highlights the cues, and stores the information for future use. Our subconscious recognizes the cues that predict specific outcomes.

A habit may begin even without you being aware of the cue. You can spot an opportunity and subconsciously do something about it. However, since your actions become automatic due to your habit, you tend to backslide into old patterns without you noticing it. The more deeply-rooted your habits are, the harder it is to change them.

You need to be aware of what your current habits are before plunging into a behavioral change.

People tasked to run the Japanese railway system observe a safety process called Pointing-and-Calling, designed to reduce errors. The system requires each train operator to use their eyes, ears, mouths, and hands to spot irregularities before they cause a problem.

When we do things automatically, we tend to omit important details. We stop asking ourselves if our action is appropriate because we act on autopilot.

One way we can be mindful of our habits is through a Habit Scorecard. First, you make a list of your daily habits. Then, tag each habit as "good," "bad," or "neutral." Good habits refer to those that reinforce your desired identity, while bad habits are those that are in conflict with who you want to become. Remember that habits are subjective; a good habit for another person may be bad for you and vice versa.

At this point, you only need to take note of your habits. Do not judge, criticize, or change any of those habits you listed.

Acknowledge your bad habits. Next time you are about to make a bad habit, say the habit and the consequence out loud to make you aware of what you are about to do.

Be aware of your habits, acknowledge the cues that trigger them, and respond in the right way.

Lessons

1. With practice, your brain spots cues that predict specific outcomes without consciously thinking about it.

2. The moment our habits become automatic, that is when we lose sight of what we are doing.

3. An awareness of your habits changes your behavior.

4. Pointing-and-Calling is a strategy that makes use of words and actions to increase your awareness of your habit.

5. The Habit Scorecard is a simple tool used to increase awareness of your behavior.

Issues Surrounding the Subject Matter

1. What are the disadvantages when you do things subconsciously because it has become a habit?

2. What are the potential problems if you are not aware of your habits?

3. Do you have a deeply-rooted habit that you find hard to change? What habit is this?

4. Think about the times where your reaction to certain events or matters was instantaneous or automatic, like polishing off that packet of potato chips before realizing you had really meant to just eat half. How did that make you feel deep down?

Goals

1. What can you do to avoid problems caused by acting on autopilot?

Action Steps

1. Prepare a Habit Scorecard to keep track of your daily habits.

2. List down other ideas on how you can keep yourself aware of your habits and how each affects you and your relationship with others.

3. Think of ways which you can utilize the Habit Scorecard practically in your daily life.

4. How can you boost your mindfulness about your habits and maintain that mindfulness?

Checklist

1. List all your daily habits from the time you wake up until you go to sleep. If there are habits that you do weekly or monthly, indicate them on the list.

2. Use your own set of legends to identify habits you find effective, ineffective, and neutral. Indicate the legend at the bottom of the page, so you do not forget what it means when you revisit the scorecard. Limit the number of habits you label as neutral.

Ch 5: The Best Way to Start a New Habit

Summary

In 2001, a study on habit formation was made. Participants were grouped into three details. The first group was tasked to monitor how often they exercised. The second group was asked to monitor their workouts and read materials that talk about exercise benefits. A third group was asked to do the same task as the second group plus formulate a plan for the date, time, and location of their exercise the following week. The first and second groups had 35 to 38 percent of their members exercising at least once a week; the third group registered 91 percent.

The third group's additional task was called implementation intention – a plan for when and where to perform the intended action.

Several cues trigger a habit, but the most common are time and location. Implementation intentions use these two cues and follow a simple format. If you are doing this for the first time, you might want to include the date when you intend to begin the habit.

" I will [Behavior] on [Date] at [Time] in [Place]."

People who use an implementation intention are more likely to succeed at habit formation. Besides providing clarity, an implementation intention helps you avoid deterrents and distractions that would hamper your habit formation.

We tend to perform an action that is connected to what we have just completed doing. Every action triggers the next. The same principle applies to habit formation. This approach, introduced by Stanford professor BJ Fogg, is called habit stacking.

Habit stacking is a variation of an implementation intention that pairs a new habit with a current habit. A simple format for this would be:

"After I [Current habit], I will [New habit].

For example, "After I eat dinner, I will update my gratitude journal."

Later, when you are comfortable with the process, you can grow your habit stack by linking small habits. Consider the following when stacking habits:

- **Timing.** Insert it a time when you are more likely to succeed. For instance, adding meditation to your early to morning routine may not be a good idea if that routine includes helping your kids prepare for and bringing them to school.

- **Frequency**. The new and current habits must have the same frequency. If you would like the new habit to be done daily, it is not wise to stack it on a habit that you do weekly.

Implementation intention and habit stacking are two strategies that support the 1st law of behavior change: make it obvious.

Lessons

1. An implementation intention is a habit formation strategy that uses the two most common triggers: time and location.

2. Habit stacking is another strategy where a new habit piggybacks on a current habit.

3. Both habit stacking and implementation intention make triggers to behavior changes noticeable.

Issues surrounding the subject matter

1. What difficulties do you face when starting a new habit?

2. Take a quiet moment to think about your daily life schedule and how you can perform habit stacking through inserting wanted habits on top of existing routines.

Goals

1. What do you intend to do to overcome the difficulties of forming a new habit?

Action Steps

1. Identify a habit you would like to develop.

2. Create an implementation intention for the selected habit.

3. Stack up the selected habit with an existing habit.

4. Add in your desired identity into the mix whilst you are working on the habits. Keep reminding yourself of that desired identity so that it becomes tied in to your selected new habits.

Checklist

1. In a previous chapter, you have identified a habit you need to form. Start with that.

2. If you are not sure when it is best to start your habit, try the first day of the week, month, or year. Choose a time of day when there are the least distractions.

3. Stack up habits with the same frequency to ensure that the new habit will get done. Ensure that the habit you are forming is stacked on an effective habit.

4. Document both your implementation intention and habit stacking strategies.

Ch 6: Motivation is Overrated; Environment Often Matters More

Summary

One of the factors that influence human behavior is our environment. According to Kurt Lewin, a psychologist, human behavior is a function of the person in their environment. This principle was tried in business. In 1952, the economist Hawkins Stern labeled a marketing strategy as Suggestion Impulse Buying. The strategy suggests that buying triggers are not always based on the customer's need or want but because of the product's visibility. Customers are prone to buy items positioned at eye level than those that are on the bottom shelf.

We perceive things based on our sense of sight, hearing, smell, taste, and touch, but the strongest of these is our sight. Since we are more dependent on our sense of sight than the other senses, visual cues are the best catalyst of behavior.

Habit formation begins with a cue, but it must be evident for us to notice it. We can leverage visual cues by designing our environment in a way that will be helpful to us. For example, if you want to drink more water, fill water bottles or jugs every morning and place them in locations where you often stay, e.g., in your workspace, bedroom, kitchen, etc.

Over time, our habits are linked with several triggers that describe the context surrounding our behavior. We have a certain relationship with our environment so that each location we are in connects to a particular habit. A study required insomniacs to go to bed only when they are tired. If they cannot sleep, they had to transfer to another room until they feel sleepy. After some time, it became easier for them to sleep when they go to bed – their brains picked up the message that sleeping is the only action allowed in the bedroom.

It is easier to form a habit in a new location because we do not have to deal with conflicting cues and current patterns. A new location need not be a different one – rearranging or redefining an existing location will do. As much as possible, do not mix contexts, so you do not mix habits. For example, if you use your kitchen counter or dining table for work, you tend to develop the habit of eating while working, which is not healthy or productive.

It is easier to form habits in an environment where every space has a specific use. Design your environment to:

- Expose positive cues and conceal negative ones

- Create stability and predictability

Lessons

1. A cue triggers each habit. The more prominent the cue is, the more likely we can form the habit.

2. Over time, our habits are triggered by several cues that form the environment or context surrounding the behavior.

3. It is easier to develop a habit in a new location because there are no existing cues to grapple with.

Issues surrounding the subject matter

1. Does your current environment encourage you to form new habits? Why or why not?

2. What problems are there if cues or habit triggers do not stand out?

3. Sometimes thinking out of the box would be very beneficial when obvious solutions to your environment do not present themselves. Take for instance eating on your working table; if you really have to do that, apportion different spaces on the working table for different uses. Designate a space for eating and the other just for working.

Goals

1. How can you make your current environment support you in forming a new habit?

Action Steps

1. Redesign your current environment so that all cues are visible.

2. Assign a space in your current environment for the habit you are forming.

Checklist

1. Refer to the habit and cues listed on the worksheet prepared from Chapter 3.

2. Document how you redesigned your environment. You may use words or pictures to document it. Include a brief explanation of why you redesigned it in that manner. You might need this information later when you add another habit to form or develop a better idea for redesigning your place.

Ch 7: The Secret of Self-Control

Summary

In 1971, US lawmakers learned that more than 15% of soldiers stationed in Vietnam were heroin addicts. Further investigation showed the problem was worse than the initial discovery – 35% of the servicemen had tried heroin, and 20% were addicted.

Those who used heroin were monitored when they returned home. Researchers found that nearly nine out of ten soldiers who used heroin in Vietnam got rid of their addiction overnight. This finding disproved the belief that heroin addiction is permanent.

While in Vietnam, the soldiers were exposed to strong context cues that led to their addiction. When they returned to their families, the significant change in their environment enabled most of them to eliminate the addiction.

The relevant studies challenged prevailing beliefs that associate bad habits with moral weakness and lack of self-discipline. Recent research reveals that people who seem to have remarkable self-control are also struggling. The only difference they have with those who are perceived to be undisciplined is knowing how to create a disciplined environment.

Habits are already programmed in our brains. We can break a bad habit, but it remains in our brain even if we do not practice it for a long time. People find it challenging to eliminate a bad habit because of a phenomenon called "cue-induced wanting": an external cue that causes an uncontrollable desire to repeat a bad habit. For example, when you pressure an obese person to lose weight, they feel stressed and cope with it by overeating.

Self-control will allow you to resist the temptation a couple of times, but it will not give you the willpower to curb your craving all the time. It is better to cut a bad habit by doing the inverse of the 1st Law of Behavior Change: make its triggers invisible, and pair them off with more exposure to triggers of good habits.

Lessons

1. Formed habits are never forgotten, even if they have not been practiced for a long time.

2. Doing the reverse of the 1st Law of Behavior Change is an effective way of breaking a bad habit: make the triggers invisible.

3. People with high self-control do not resist temptation – they avoid it.

Issues surrounding the subject matter

1. Do you have a bad habit that you find difficult to break? What makes it so?

2. Bringing mindfulness about your thoughts and actions to the fore can also help with arresting the impulse toward bad habits. Reflect on the times when you are about to do something you will regret, yet you catch yourself with that thought and that was sufficient to at least halt the impulse. You can recall these instances with regards to the bad habits that you want to kick and note them down in a journal for daily reflection if you wish.

Goals

1. What bad habit would you like to break free from? What do you intend to do about it?

Action Steps

1. Identify the bad habit that you like to break.

2. Re-assess your environment. If needed, redesign it.

3. List down ways to make your bad habit's triggers invisible. Below are some examples:

a. Stop buying junk food/cigarettes/soda. Skip the grocery lane where the shelves of these items are.

b. Uninstall all unnecessary apps from your phone, laptop, tablet, etc.

c. Limit your subscriptions to only those necessary

Checklist

1. Refer to the bad habit listed on the Habit Scorecard from Chapter 4.

2. In the previous chapter, you redesigned your environment to expose the cues for your good habits. Check if the existing design can conceal the triggers of your bad habits. The less change you do with the design, the better.

PART THREE: THE 2ND LAW: MAKE IT ATTRACTIVE

Ch 8: How to Make a Habit Irresistible

<u>Summary</u>

In the 1940s, scientist Niko Tinbergen performed experiments that altered beliefs on what motivates people. There is a small red dot on the beak of adult herring gulls. Newly hatched chicks would peck on this dot each time they wanted food. Tinbergen created cardboard beaks, each with a red dot. When the adult gulls had flown away, Tinbergen brought the fake beaks to the chicks who pecked at the red dot. The bigger the dot, the faster they pecked.

The same behavior was observed in the greylag goose. As the mother moves around the nest, an egg will roll out, settling on the grass. The mother will pull it back into the nest. Tinbergen observed that the mother did the same thing for any round object that she will find on the grass nearby.

The baby gulls and the greylag goose were acting on instinct. Their brains are programmed with rules of behavior to which they respond strongly when the rule is amplified. These amplified cues are called supernormal stimuli.

Like these animals, humans are easily taken in by exaggerated versions of things and circumstances. Food science focuses on making products more attractive to consumers, so they spend much to discover how to create the ideal mouthfeel and dynamic contrast their food products present. The better the mouthfeel and the higher the contrast, the more we crave for that food product; the more we crave, the higher the possibility of developing the habit of overeating.

If you want to develop a habit, you need to apply the 2nd Law of Behavior Change: make it attractive. We start by understanding how craving works.

In 1954, a study made by neuroscientists revealed that the absence of dopamine destroyed craving, and without craving, there was no action. The higher the dopamine level, the stronger the craving, and the action became faster and consistent.

Dopamine was initially thought to be about pleasure. Still, the study indicated that it plays a crucial role in several neurological processes such as motivation, voluntary movement, learning, memory, aversion, and punishment.

Dopamine is released when you experience pleasure and when you anticipate it. When you anticipate the pleasure, the level of dopamine spikes, boosting your motivation to experience the pleasure. Often, the pleasure in anticipation is more than experiencing it. Scientists say that this explains the difference between wanting and liking.

Making the triggers attractive leads us to anticipate and want the rewarding experience and prompts us to make the experience happen. One strategy for making the trigger attractive is known as temptation bundling.

Temptation bundling is combining an action you need to do with what you want to do. This strategy, used by most businesses, is an application of Premack's Principle: "more probable behaviors will reinforce less probable behaviors."

For example, Ronan Byrne, an electrical engineering student, reconfigured his stationary bike to connect to his laptop and television. He programmed the entire system such that Netflix will only run if his bicycle runs at a certain speed. Slowing down meant pausing whatever show he was watching.

A more practical way of using temptation bundling is combining it with habit stacking:

1. After I [Current Habit], I will [Habit I need]

2. After I [Habit I need], I will [Habit I want]

For example, if you enjoy watching TV, you may write:

After I eat breakfast, I will clean my room.

After I clean my room, I will watch TV.

The habit you need becomes the trigger for the habit you want. This approach makes you look forward to doing the habit you need because it means you get to do what you want.

If heightened versions of reality spur us to action, temptation bundling is a heightened version of any habit we can use to make habits more attractive.

Lessons

1. People are more likely to form a habit when the trigger and the expected reward are attractive.

2. It is not experiencing the reward that propels us to develop a habit – it is the anticipation of the reward. The more we anticipate it, the higher our dopamine level becomes.

3. As dopamine increases, so does our motivation to act.

4. Temptation bundling is putting together an action you want with an action you need. It is a strategy to make habits more attractive.

Issues surrounding the subject matter

1. What problems does a supernormal stimulus present?

2. Do you have a habit that you find challenging to do or maintain? What causes the difficulty?

Goals

1. How do you make your difficult habit attractive?

2. How do you make a new habit you are forming more appealing?

Action Steps

1. Identify a difficult habit that you need to do.

2. Identify a habit you enjoy doing.

3. Prepare two temptation bundling statements: one, for the difficult habit and two, for the new habit you are forming.

Checklist

1. Refer to your Habit Scorecard to identify the habit you enjoy doing.

2. Go back to the worksheet you prepared from Chapter 3 for the new habit you are forming.

3. Use the habit stack you did in Chapter 5 to do the temptation bundle.

Ch 9: The Role of Family and Friends in Shaping Your Habits

Summary

Humans have a deep-seated desire to belong.

Our first habits were not our choice – they were handed down to us by our family, our teachers, and the society we moved into during our early years. We imitated some of our habits from our friends and the community we belonged to. They became the norms that guided our behavior, and we followed them blindly and mindlessly because it gave us a sense of belonging.

We tend to imitate the habits of three groups: the close, the many, and the powerful. Each group makes those habits more attractive.

1. The Close

We pick up habits of people who surround us, consciously or unconsciously. The closer we are to a person, the greater our tendency to mimic their habits. People close to us seem to give us tacit peer pressure to adopt their ways. However, this tendency can be a problem if we are around people with bad habits.

One way of developing better habits is to connect with people or groups whose normal behavior mirrors your desired behavior. New habits seem attainable and appealing when you see people you are with doing it regularly. It even becomes more attractive when you share something in common with these people.

Your growth becomes more meaningful when shared with others, and the shared identity bolsters your identity.

2. The Many

In the 1950s, psychologist Solomon Asch conducted a social experiment that proved that a person is likely to agree with the majority even if they see, feel, or think differently. When we doubt our actions, we rely on the group to guide our behavior. We feel secure when our choices are aligned with the group.

However, there is a drawback to this tendency. We all want to relate well with others, and in so wanting, we tend to adopt their norms and refuse to challenge them even if we know they are wrong. Changing for the better becomes unattractive, and that deters us from developing good habits.

3. The Powerful

It is human nature to want praise, recognition, and respect, which explains why many people pursue power, status, and prestige. We take an interest in the success stories of well-known people, and we adopt habits of people we respect and admire.

We get attracted to behaviors that earn us the approval and praise of other people, especially those we hold in high regard. We avoid behaviors that will lower other people's opinions about us. Our behavior is based on how we want other people to see us.

Lessons

1. We embrace the habits of people close to us, the society, and the powerful because we like to belong and gain the respect and approval of these people.

2. An effective way of developing better habits is to be a part of a culture whose normal behavior is the same as our desired behavior and share something in common.

3. The downside of being a part of a culture is our tendency to blindly accept their norms even when we think differently.

4. Behaviors that bring us praise, approval, and respect appeal to us.

Issues surrounding the subject matter

1. What are the downsides to imitating the habits of people close to you, e.g., family and friends? Of people

within your community and society in general? Of powerful people?

2. Were you ever in a situation where you had to compromise your value, opinion, and decisions because you opted to join the majority? How did it feel? What do you think would have happened if you stood by your conviction?

3. Do you still have habits handed down to you by your family, teachers, or friends? What are these habits? Why are you keeping them?

Goals

1. How would you like to have habits that reflect the real you and not because it was imposed on you or because you gave in to pressure?

2. Take a moment to recall that desirous identity which we did a while back ago in the previous chapters. Ponder about the traits which you wish to develop as well as the habits which would be needed in order for you to achieve your goal.

Action Steps

1. Identify habits that you picked up or mimicked from your network, those you do because of your affiliation

with a group, or because you were under pressure to do it. Mark them.

2. Evaluate each marked habit: is it something you would have done on your own because it supports your desired identity? If you answered no, mark the habit with another symbol to indicate that you need to assess the habit further.

3. Assess the remaining habits and assess if they are sufficient to build your desired identity. If not, decide whether you would like to introduce a new habit or bring back one from those identified for further assessment.

Checklist

1. Refer to your Habit Scorecard.

2. Opposite the items you marked for further assessment, indicate why you did so. Transfer these items to a separate sheet of paper, if necessary.

Ch 10: How to Find and Fix the Causes of Your Bad Habits

Summary

Our craving expresses our hidden core motive. When we crave a cigarette, our motive is not to smoke but relieve us from stress. If you look closely, you will find there is nothing new with the underlying motives. These are the same cravings generations before you have been wanting; however, the habits that meet these wants have changed. For example, Gen Z satisfies their need to connect with others through Facebook, baby boomers through get-togethers.

There are several ways to deal with the same underlying motive. One might smoke to relieve stress, and others might opt for meditation, running, shopping, etc. When an action succeeds at dealing with the underlying motive, we crave to repeat the action.

As our brain picks up cues, it predicts our next action based on relevant knowledge or experience. For example, when we notice that the stove is on, we know it is hot and predicts that we will get burned if we touch it; our action is to refrain from touching it.

Our behavior depends mostly on predictions or how we interpret events that happen to us. These predictions lead to feelings, which prompt us to act. When we crave to fill the gap between where we are and where we want to be, we are compelled to act.

Some habits are harder to form and maintain, so we tend to avoid them. But if we associate it with a positive experience, it becomes more attractive and worth pursuing. A slight change in mindset will also be helpful. For example, when you think that you "have to" do something, you see the act as an obligation. But if you think of it as something that you "get" to do, you begin to look at it as an opportunity. When we emphasize the benefits of our habits instead of looking at its downsides, our habit becomes more attractive.

Design your motivation ritual. Connect your habits with something you enjoy, then use that as a cue. Ed Latimore, a boxer and writer, would put on his headphones to listen to his brand of music while writing. Later, putting on his headphones became his cue to focus on his writing – even when there was no music.

Lessons

1. Each behavior has a surface level motive, which we know as craving, and a more profound underlying motive.

2. The underlying motives may be the same across generations, but the habits developed to address them vary for each generation.

3. When we spot cues, our brain predicts what will happen. This prediction leads to feelings that drive us to action.

4. Difficult habits become attractive when linked with positive feelings. Design a motivation ritual that allows you to do something you delight in immediately after a problematic habit.

5. Change your mindset to make difficult habits more attractive. Make bad habits unattractive so you can break them.

Issues surrounding the subject matter

1. What are the downsides to having a motivation ritual?

2. What were your cravings for your bad habits?

3. There is always a positive side to every, single thing in life. Should the good habit seem particularly tough to do, you can try to focus on the good part of it, so that it boost your intent to act. Some people might find the act of giving tough; these folks can cultivate the thought process that the opportunity to give may not always be

present, so when they have the chance to give, they should jump at it! This can be applied to most things.

Goals

1. How would you like to address the underlying motives of your cravings with good habits?

2. What would it take for you to make a problematic habit consistently?

Action Steps

1. Think through your desires that led to your bad habits. Identify the underlying motives for these cravings.

    a. For each motive, ask yourself: "Is this the only way to satisfy this motive?"

    b. Explore possibilities and list them down next to each motive. Limit the list to good habits.

    c. Based on your list, identify an action that would satisfy the most number of motives—plan on having this action formed into a habit if this is not part of your habits yet.

2. Design your motivation ritual.

Checklist

1. Refer to the list of habits in your Habit Scorecard.

PART FOUR: THE 3RD LAW: MAKE IT EASY

Ch 11: Walk Slowly, but Never Backward

Summary

We give too much focus on coming up with the best plan for change, but we never get to execute it.

Motion and action are different. Motion is all about planning and learning but does not produce the result, while action delivers results. Motion is useful, but without action, it will not generate the result.

Sometimes, we prefer to be in motion because it delays failure while giving us some semblance of progress. It is just a preparation for the action required. Being in motion can be a form of procrastination.

Habit formation does not require perfection but a repetitive execution of the action so that behavior becomes automatic. All habits follow the same path that begins with a conscious effort to practice the behavior until it reaches automaticity or the stage at which we subconsciously carry out the behavior.

People are interested in finding out how long it takes to form a new habit. However, it is the frequency of execution or the number of repetitions of the behavior that allows us to develop a new habit. What is more important is to take all necessary action to progress into forming a new habit. To do this, you need to apply the 3rd Law of Behavior Change: Make it Easy.

Lessons

1. Habits are formed by doing, not planning.

2. Habit formation requires constant repetition of behavior until it becomes automatic.

3. The frequency of action is more important than the length of time you have been practicing the habit.

Issues surrounding the subject matter

1. Why is it not practical to plan your habits?

2. What hitches do you see happening when you focus on the length of time you practice the habit?

3. Do you foresee a problem in implementing the new habit you are forming? What is the problem, and what is its cause?

Goals

1. How do you intend to form your desired new habit work for you effectively?

Action Steps

1. Assess the frequency of repetition of the habit.

2. Reinforce the use of habit stacking and implementation intention.

Checklist

1. Refer to the following:

    a. The worksheet prepared from Chapter 3

    b. The implementation intention written from Chapter 5

    c. The habit stacking statement written from Chapter 5

Ch 12: The Law of Least Effort

Summary

Motivation drives us to change our habits. However, humans are naturally motivated by what is convenient. Our brains are programmed to conserve energy, so we follow the Law of Least Effort: given two options, we are inclined to choose the one that requires less work and effort.

When you start your exercise regimen, you might be tempted to aim for a hundred push-ups daily. While you might succeed because of your excitement, you will easily get drained on the succeeding days.

Our habit is an obstruction to what we want. We are forming the habit not because of the habit itself but because of its results. The more complicated the habit, the more we resist it; it becomes crucial to make the habit easy.

Environment design, a strategy used to make cues obvious, is also helpful in making a habit easy. Habits are easier to develop if the action is already a part of the flow of your life. For example, it is easier to regularly go to the gym if it is located along your daily route.

Lessen the sources of resistance within your home or your office. Eliminate the points of friction that waste your time and weaken energy so you can do more with less effort. For example, having ready-to-eat meals frees you from the friction of having to buy groceries and cooking meals. Redesign your environment to make a good habit convenient to practice.

Use each space for its real purpose and organize it to prepare it for the next activity. Be creative in finding ways to prime your environment. If you want to do an early morning jog, bring your jogging outfit from your closet and lay them down at the foot of your bed, so you do not have to prepare them upon waking up.

The reverse can be applied to avoid bad habits. Add as much friction as possible to discourage you from practicing the habit. For example, when you need to focus on your work, keep your mobile phone where you cannot easily reach it so you will not be tempted to check your social media.

Make meaningful actions easy to do.

Lessons

1. We lean towards options that require less time and effort.

2. Design your environment to make good habits convenient and easy to do and bad habits requiring more time and energy.

Issues surrounding the subject matter

1. Why is it not advisable to do more than one habit in the same space even if the habits are stacked?

2. Have you been tempted to skip a new habit because just the thought of it has wearied you? Why did you feel that way?

Goals

1. What will you do to ensure that you keep to your new habit?

Action Steps

1. Check how the new habit can be a part of the regular flow of your daily activities.

2. Re-assess how your environment is designed. Does it make it easy for you to perform your new habit? If not, redesign your home and office space.

3. Spot and eliminate time wasters that impact your new habit.

4. Prime your environment. Organize the space where you perform your new habit.

Checklist

1. Refer to the habit you identified in Chapter 3.

2. Document how you redesigned your environment, like how you did in Chapter 6.

Ch 13: How to Stop Procrastinating by Using the Two-Minute Rule

<u>Summary</u>

About 40 to 50% of what we do daily are habit-driven. Habits are subconscious choices that prompt our willful decisions. Although they only take a few seconds to execute, habits can significantly influence our future actions.

Daily, we experience decisive moments that spell enormous impact on how our day will turn out. Decisive moments are the little choices we make that pile up within the day and yield new sets of choices that shape our next moves.

Going into a restaurant is a decisive moment that determines what you will eat for dinner. Although you decide what you order, you are constrained by what the place offers. Your choice of a restaurant controls your options.

In habit formation, it is easy to attempt to do too much too soon. This tendency can be addressed by the Two-Minute Rule, which says that it should only take less than two minutes to execute when starting a new habit. Our target is to make each habit easy to begin so that once we have started to practice it, the habit becomes easier to maintain. This is referred to as the "gateway" habit. For example, instead of aiming for a 3-mile run, you can cut it back to "tie my running shoes."

Categorize your goals into a range that goes from "very easy" to "very hard," as shown in the table below.

Very Easy	Easy	Moderate	Hard	Very Hard
Put on running shoes	Walk 2x around the block	Walk around the village	Run 10 miles	Run a marathon
Read one page	Read five pages	Read one chapter	Read five chapters	Read an entire book

Those under the "Very Easy" column are the gateway habits that will ultimately lead you to habits classified as "Very Hard." You can complete these gateway habits within two minutes. The Two-Minute Rule is not intended to start the process of habit formation; it is a strategy for reinforcing your identity. What you do within the first two minutes is the habit that you must develop.

When you have established the habit, the Two-Minute Rule may be paired off with a technique called habit shaping to move your habit a notch higher toward your goal. Like the gateway habit, you master the first phase before moving on to the next level. For example, when you want to become a vegan, you can shape your habit as follows:

Phase 1: Eat vegetables at each meal.

Phase 2: Do not eat the meat of four-legged animals.

Phase 3: Stop eating the meat of two-legged animals.

Phase 4: Avoid eating the meat of animals with no legs.

Phase 5: Stop eating all animal products, e.g., eggs, cheese, milk

When you find yourself wrestling with a habit, apply the Two-Minute Rule to make the habit easy. Do it slowly if you must. What is more important is you applying the habits you have identified for yourself.

Lessons

1. Habits can be completed quickly, but their effects on your behavior last long.

2. Countless habits take place during decisive moments, and they can either make your day constructive or unproductive.

3. The Two-Minute Rule requires us to scale down our habit into something we can complete in two minutes.

Issues surrounding the subject matter

1. Why do you think we are discouraged from doing something a bit ambitious, e.g., run 3 miles on the first day, when we start a habit?

2. Have your tried starting a new habit with something a bit complicated or time-consuming? How did it end up?

3. Have you experienced a decisive moment and made a choice which you realized later was not helpful to your habit formation? What happened?

Goals

1. How do you intend to make your new habit easy to do?

Action Steps

1. Scale down your desired habit into two-minute activities. Categorize it based on the level of complexity, from very easy to very hard. Begin doing the most effortless activity until it becomes a habit, then move to the next level. Do the same for each level.

2. When confronted with a decisive moment, ask yourself, "Will this help me in my habit formation?" If not, skip the action and look for alternatives.

Checklist

1. Work on the habit you identified in Chapter 3.

2. Document the scaled-down activities.

Ch 14: How to Make Good Habits Inevitable and Bad Habits Impossible

Summary

Success is not always about making good habits easy; sometimes, it is more of making bad habits challenging, which is the inverse of the 3rd Law of Behavior Change. One way of doing this is what is known in psychology as a commitment device.

A commitment device is a deliberate choice to compel you to practice good habits and restrain you from doing bad ones. It allows you to leverage on good intentions before you succumb to temptation and raises the probability that you will do the right thing in the future by making the bad habits challenging in the present.

There are numerous ways to make a commitment device. The key is to alter the activity so that it requires more effort to dodge the good habit than to initiate it. For example, you get an additional 30 minutes of TV per night when you practice your habit and no TV when you don't. Other examples include going to a place where there is no internet access so you can focus on your job and paying the annual gym membership fee upfront so you will be compelled to go to the gym regularly.

It is best to break a bad habit by increasing the friction until it is practically impossible to do. These can be done through one-time choices that may require effort at the start but pays off over time as they lock in good habits. Examples of these one-time actions would include buying a good mattress to encourage good sleeping habits, putting your phone on silent mode so you can focus on your work, cut cable service to save on money, etc.

Automation is one way of eliminating bad habits and promoting the good ones. It allows you to focus your resources on activities that machines cannot do yet. This approach is useful for infrequently practiced behaviors becoming habitual, e.g., automatic salary deduction to save for retirement.

However, technology can work against us. It offers you the convenience to give in to your cravings so that you can go from one easy task to another. The more difficult but rewarding activities are often put aside.

Commitment devices, technology, and one-time actions create an environment where good habits are failsafe.

Lessons

1. Making the habit difficult allows you to break bad habits.

2. Commitment devices, technology, and one-time actions lock in good behavior and make bad habits impossible.

Issues surrounding the subject matter

1. What problems do you foresee in using automation to eliminate bad habits?

2. Do you see any conflict in applying one-time actions to make the habit easy? What are these?

3. Think about the times when you have been put off from developing good habits because of the sheer amount of effort required to perform them. Apply that same line of thought into creating barriers of friction to the bad habits you are trying to kick. If you are trying to wean off ice cream, prevent yourself from going to the ice cream section of the store. You can think out of the box when coming up with ideas to build or ease friction.

Goals

1. What will make it easy for you to do good habits?

2. What will discourage you from doing bad habits?

Action Steps

1. Automate your habits. When possible, invest in technology.

2. Do one-time actions that will help you keep your good habits and break the bad ones.

3. Create commitment devices to discourage bad behavior.

Checklist

1. Continue working on the habit you identified in Chapter 3.

2. Check the internet for apps and similar technology that will help you with your habit formation.

3. Research on applications of commitment devices to get ideas on what will work for you.

PART FIVE:
THE 4TH LAW: MAKE IT SATISFYING

Ch 15: The Cardinal Rule of Behavior Change

Summary

We are more inclined to repeat a behavior when the experience is enjoyable. When we are delighted and satisfied after doing something, our brain tells us to do it again. On the other hand, if the experience is not gratifying, we do not see any reason to repeat it. Further, we need to immediately experience the reward; otherwise, it diminishes the satisfaction level of doing the habit. This relationship between reward and habits describes the Cardinal Rule of Behavior Change: we repeat what is immediately rewarded and avoid what is immediately punished.

The first three laws of behavior change increase the possibility of performing the behavior in the present. The 4th law increases the odds of repeating the behavior, completing the habit loop.

Our ancestors lived in an immediate-return environment where they value instant gratification because of their need to survive. Society has changed several generations after, yet the way the human brain functions remain the same. We still value the reward we get now more than what can happen in the future. Our preference for immediate satisfaction leads to problems.

The rewards of bad habits are instant, but their consequences are delayed. This explains why people smoke despite the risk of lung cancer. It gives them immediate relief for their stress, but they will feel its effect on their health years later.

The immediate outcome of our bad habits are pleasurable, but the ultimate result is unpleasant. With good habits, the immediate effect is displeasing, but the ultimate consequence is rewarding.

We all plan to become better versions of ourselves, but in a decisive moment, our brain tells us to focus on the present, so we choose the path of instant gratification. Unfortunately, research has shown us that success comes to people who do better at delaying gratification.

If you want to keep a good habit, you must make its outcome rewarding. You need reinforcement that links your habit to an immediate reward that makes you fulfilled when forming a good habit. Immediate reinforcements are especially advantageous when you need to avoid certain behaviors.

One technique of dealing with that is to make the avoidance visible. For example, open an account and label it for something you badly want, e.g., a trip overseas. Each time you avoid buying junk food, put a certain amount into that special savings account. When you are down to your desired weight, you can enjoy your trip as a reward.

However, be sure that your choice of reinforcement will support your desired identity and not bring you back to where you started. For example, if you want to keep a healthy habit, do not reward yourself with having dinner at a classy steakhouse.

Let your desired identity become the reinforcer. The more a good habit becomes natural to you, the less reinforcement you will need. Incentives drive you to start a habit, but it is your identity that will sustain it.

A habit should be pleasurable for it to stick. Use simple reinforcements that align with your identity to make you enjoy the habit.

Lessons

1. We are more apt to repeat a behavior when the experience is gratifying.

2. The 4th Law of Behavior Change – make it satisfying – bolsters the chances of repeating the behavior.

3. The Cardinal Rule of Behavior Change states that we repeat whatever is immediately rewarded; we avoid whatever is immediately punished.

4. Small, simple reinforcements that align with your identity will help you sustain a good habit.

Issues surrounding the subject matter

1. What is the problem with having our brain focused on the present?

2. What are the challenges of making a good habit rewarding if the positive consequences are not experienced until much later?

3. Do you experience any form of gratification with the new habit you are currently forming? If yes, what is this? Is it enough to make you want to continue with it?

Goals

1. How do you intend to make your new habit pleasurable?

Action Steps

1. Use reinforcements like a commitment device that uses a reward and punishment technique.

2. Bring your habit stacking strategy to the next level.

Checklist

1. Continue working on the habit you identified in Chapter 3.

2. Review the last habit stacking statement you did and reinforce it.

Ch 16: How to Stick with Good Habits Every Day

Summary

We feel good when we progress with our goals, and having visual evidence of that progress adds to the pleasant feeling; the visual evidence reinforces the behavior. There are countless forms of visual measurements, but the best way to monitor your progress is through a habit tracker.

The calendar is the most basic tracker. You simply cross off each day that you followed your routine. After some time, you will see how far you have gone with your habit.

Habit tracking is a potent tool as it capitalizes on the Laws of Behavior Change.

Habit tracking is:

Obvious. It creates visual cues that urge you to repeat the behavior and prevent you from lying to yourself.

Attractive. The more "X's you see on the calendar, the more fulfilled you become, and the more you become motivated to maintain the habit. You would not want to break the chain of "X"s.

Satisfying. Crossing off a date on the calendar is by itself a reward. It makes you more focused on the process rather than the result.

Further, habit tracking provides visual evidence of how you are getting to be the person you want to be.

However, some people fend off the idea of tracking. They see tracking as another habit they need to develop and find the process tedious. But there are ways to simplify tracking.

Automate. Unconsciously, you are already tracking some of your habits. For example, your credit card statement records the number of times you ate out. Check out apps that help you track your habits. Review it weekly or monthly.

Limit tracking to your most critical habits.

Record each measurement immediately after performing the habit. Pair off your habit tracking with the habit stacking strategy.

> "After I [Current Habit], I will [Track my habit]"

Your habit streak will end at some point, e.g., you got sick, a family member needed you to spend more time with them, changing work demands, etc. When this happens, go back immediately to the habit. As much as possible, do not miss your habit twice in a row.

Do not fall into the all-or-nothing trap. You may slip up but what matters most is how you recover from it.

Do not be driven by the numbers. Focus instead on the purpose of tracking your progress. Choosing the wrong measurement leads us to wrong behaviors. With the hype on being data-driven, we fail to factor in things that may not be quantifiable but are equally, if not more, meaningful.

For example, your bathroom scale may be showing numbers not to your liking. But if you focus on other things like fewer occasions of negative self-talk or having better skin, you will still see your progress and be motivated by the changes you are experiencing.

Lessons

1. We feel more motivated when we know we are making progress.

2. Habit tracking provides visual proof of our progress in forming a habit.

3. Do not break the chain, nor miss the habit twice. Do not worry if you slip up but be sure to go back to your habit immediately.

4. Progress is not always about numbers. Look for other obvious cues of your progress.

Issues surrounding the subject matter

1. Why do you think some people do not favor habit tracking?

2. As you track your progress, why is too much focus on numbers not advisable?

3. Have you experienced a habit chain break? How did it feel? What did you do about

4. What did you learn from the experience?

Goals

1. What can you do to stick to your good habits?

Action Steps

1. Identify the critical habits you would like to track.

2. Decide on a tracking method. Will you automate or use a manual tracker?

3. Write a habit stacking + habit tracking statement.

4. Go beyond the numbers. Look for other signs of progress that can motivate you.

Checklist

1. Refer to your Habit Scorecard to identify critical habits.

2. Check the internet for options on habit tracking.

Ch 17: How an Accountability Partner Can Change Everything

Summary

We avoid experiences that would end up being painful. The more painful the expected consequences are, the more we try to correct the situation. Without pain, we tend to ignore failure, mistakes, or bad behavior.

If you want to eliminate bad habits, you need to induce immediate pain and increase the cost of doing the bad habit. However, the cost must match the strength of the behavior that is being corrected. The consequences must be significant enough to make you want to change.

The government uses laws and ordinances to change the citizens' habits through a social contract; the citizens become accountable for their actions.

You can apply the same concept by creating a habit contract – a verbal or written agreement where you commit to a habit, stating your punishment if you do not stick to the habit. When the habit contract is there, ask one or two people to be your accountability partners who will sign off on the contract with you.

The habit contract may be intimidating to some, but at least keep the accountability partners. Having someone watching you and calling you out for skipping a habit can motivate and help you avoid procrastination.

Lessons

1. We become averse to repeating a bad habit if it is painful and unpleasant.

2. A habit contract helps us stick to our habit because the cost of violating it is painful.

3. Having accountability partners creates an immediate cost when we skip our habit.

Issues surrounding the subject matter

1. What are the downsides of using a habit contract to ensure accountability?

2. What makes accountability crucial to habit formation?

Goals

1. What will you do to hold yourself accountable for your habits?

Action Steps

1. Ask two people you trust to be your accountability partners.

2. Draft a habit contract to specify what your liabilities are when you fail to keep your habit.

3. Sign off on the contract

Checklist

1. Make the contract simple.

2. Choose reasonable penalties that will induce pain should you break from your good habit.

PART SIX:
ADVANCED TACTICS
HOW TO GO FROM BEING MERELY GOOD TO BEING TRULY GREAT

Ch 18: The Truth About Talent (When Genes Matter and When They Don't)

Summary

Habits that associate with our natural inclinations and abilities are easier to perform and more rewarding. Knowing these, we need to understand the role our genes play in developing our talents and abilities.

We cannot change genes, and while they may benefit us in some circumstances, our genes can also be a severe drawback in others. For example, being tall will be useful when you want to play basketball but may be a disadvantage if you want to go into horse racing or auto racing.

Our environment defines the suitability of our genes and the value of our natural physical and mental abilities. If you want to succeed, the selection of the habit you want to develop is crucial.

Genes do not determine our future, but they help us identify opportunities. To identify these opportunities and the right habits, we need to peek into your personality.

Our genes influence everything about us – the decisions we make, how we react to situations, etc. Our unique cluster of genetic traits gives us our unique personality or set of characteristics that we manifest consistently in any situation. Personality traits are itemized into five behavioral bands, known as the "Big Five."

Openness to experience: Cautious and consistent on one end and curious and inventive on the other end

Conscientiousness: From organized and efficient to spontaneous and laidback

Extroversion: From introverted and distant to outgoing and lively

Agreeableness: From detached and difficult to compassionate and friendly

Neuroticism: From anxious and sensitive to calm, stable, and confident

Build habits that work for your personality, instead of those that are popular or what others say you should. Shaping your habits to your personality is a good start, but you can do more when you find opportunities that will work to your advantage.

Use the explore/exploit trade-off strategy. This strategy is a trial-and-error process requiring you to explore possibilities, look into a broad spectrum of ideas, and select the best option. Stick with what delivers the results about 80 to 90% of the time and explore some more with the rest.

The extent of exploration will also depend on the amount of time you have. If you do not have much time, you need to choose and implement the best solution so far. You can streamline your options by asking yourself the following questions:

What do I find fun to do but feels like work to others? You do not necessarily have to love it, but you need to know if you can deal with the pain attached to it better than other people.

What makes me lose track of time? When you become focused on the task and lose yourself in it, you experience a balance of joy and peak performance that leaves you satisfied.

Where do I gain more than the average person? If we know that we are doing better than others, we become more motivated.

What comes naturally to me? Focus on yourself. Forget what you have been taught or told. What engages you the most?

If you cannot be better than others, try to be different so you can stand out. Master a specific skill so you can specialize in it.

We cannot use our genes as an excuse to skip hard work. They tell us what our strengths are and what to work harder on. They help us understand our nature so we can adopt an appropriate success strategy. Know your limits and deal with them.

Lessons

1. Choosing the right habit makes our progress easy; choosing the wrong habit makes us struggle.

2. We cannot change our genes. They work to our benefit in certain circumstances but becomes a disadvantage in others.

3. Pick habits that fit your personality – they are easier to develop.

4. Take advantage of your strengths. Create opportunities that will highlight your strengths.

5. Our genes do not reduce the need to work hard. They tell us what we need to work hard on.

Issues surrounding the subject matter

1. What is wrong with forming a widespread habit?

2. What problems do you expect to experience when you pick a habit that does not fit your personality?

Goals

1. In what way can you become a better version of yourself?

Action Steps

1. Form habits that work for your personality. They will be useful in building your desired identity.

2. Apply the explore/exploit trade-off strategy. Streamline options using the five questions specified above to ensure peak performance.

3. Master a specific skill you can specialize in.

Checklist

1. If you do not have the luxury of time to explore extensively, work with whatever options you have. You can look into other options later.

Ch 19: The Goldilocks Rule; How to Stay Motivated in Life and Work

Summary

A scientific study revealed that people sustain a high motivation level when they work on manageable challenges. The human brain continually seeks challenges, but if it becomes too difficult, your motivation level diminishes; a too-easy task will make you lose interest.

You are more invested in a challenge of manageable difficulty where you have a good chance of only winning if you work hard for it. This embodies the Goldilocks Rule, which says that people are motivated the most when they work within their current abilities with just the right level of difficulty.

When you have established a habit, do not stop there. Continue to improve yourself in small ways to keep you engaged and experience a flow state that is being engrossed and "in the zone." Do not stop looking for challenges that push you to your limits but keep you motivated. Try for variety to avoid boredom, which is the biggest adversary of self-improvement.

Practice leads to mastery, but the longer you practice, the more boring and tedious the activity becomes. Boredom poses the biggest threat to your success. You start seeking something new when it hits you, effectively derailing your progress with the original activity. Experiencing something novel rewards you with continual elements of surprise, which psychologists refer to as a variable reward.

At some point, our habits will become boring. When you stick to a habit, you will reach a point when you feel like quitting. But what sets apart a successful person is their ability to step up when it is painful to do so. Embrace boredom. Stick to your habit regardless of your mood. It is your route to excellence.

Lessons

1. Based on the Goldilocks Rule, people are highly motivated when working on tasks aligned with their current abilities and provide the right amount of challenge.

2. Boredom, which is the biggest threat to success, sets in when a habit becomes routine and automatic.

3. People work hard with the right motivation. Those who step up when the task becomes tedious and tiresome stand out from the rest.

Issues surrounding the subject matter

1. What are the consequences if you practice a skill or a habit to acquire mastery? Why is that bad?

2. Have you experienced boredom? What caused it? How did it affect you? How did you get out of it?

Goals

1. What will you do to keep yourself motivated?

Action Steps

1. Continuously look for new habits to form.

2. If possible, introduce something new to your routine. For example, if you have been eating breakfast in your kitchen, you may break the monotony by doing it on the patio.

3. Acquire a new hobby.

4. Make new friends.

5. Learn something new.

6. Be in the company of positive-minded people.

7. So many other ways to keep yourself motivated

Checklist

1. The idea is for you to step up no matter how dreary the situation may be. You have the power to reverse it.

Ch 20: The Downside of Creating Good Habits

Summary

Habits enable mastery, and they are the pillars of the quest for excellence. When you have mastered tasks such as ingrained in your subconscious, you can shift your focus to more challenging tasks. However, the downside to mastery is the tendency to forego feedback, go about the task mechanically, and stop spotting errors. Over time, mastery of skill leads to a slight drop in performance, which should be alright when referring to trivial tasks such as brewing coffee.

However, when you want to expand your potential and achieve peak performance, you cannot rely on habits alone. You need to pair them off with deliberate practice to achieve mastery. Each habit that you master prompts you to master another habit and internalize a new skill. It is an ongoing process that intends to create a better you.

Avoid the complacency trap. Reflect and review on what you have accomplished and what you are currently doing. This process allows you to see your mistakes and consider how you can do better. Without it, you will not know if you are doing better or worse; you can rationalize your mistakes, make excuses, and even lie to yourself.

Design your reflection and review process, but you might want to start with the following reflection questions:

- What went well?

- What could have gone better?

- What did I learn?

Establish the frequency of your reflection and review. Better yet, calendar it.

Always link your reflection with your identity. At the start, you developed a habit to achieve your desired identity. However, achieving that new identity can work against you. If you take pride in your new identity, you might deny having weaknesses, and that will prevent you from growing.

The more attached we are to our identity, the stronger our desire to shield it from criticism. One way of avoiding this pitfall is to stop making a single aspect of your identity define who you are; otherwise, you fade along with it when that aspect fades. For example, if a military man defines himself as a soldier, how would he feel when his period of service ends?

Latch on to essential aspects of your identity that will not change with your current role. Instead of defining yourself as a soldier, you can describe yourself as a person who is reliable, disciplined, and a team player.

Habits are good for us, but they can also trap us into old ways of thinking and acting even as life changes. A regular reflection and review will help us see if our habits are still useful.

Lessons

1. Habits allow us to act on autopilot, but they also stop us from seeing our weak spots.

2. Mastery of a habit or skill can be acquired by pairing off habits with deliberate practice.

3. A regular reflection and review is a reflective process that keeps us aware of our strengths and improvement areas.

4. The more attached we are to our identity, the more we become defensive about it, slowing down our growth in the process.

Issues surrounding the subject matter

1. What are the disadvantages of mastering a habit or a skill?

2. How can achieve your desired identity work against you?

Goals

1. What can you do to avoid complacency?

Action Steps

1. Decide on the frequency of your self-reflection and review.

2. Assess how close or how far you are to your desired identity. Evaluate the habits you have mastered.

3. Reflect on what you have achieved.

4. Take the necessary action.

Checklist

1. The frequency of reflection and review should allow a reasonable time for you to have accomplished something. You might want to do it monthly.

2. In Chapter 2, you described who you want to be. Use that worksheet to reflect on your identity.

3. Use the guide questions contained in this chapter summary to reflect. However, these are guide questions. You may use other guide questions like, "How do I make things better?", "What action should I take?" etc.

Conclusion:
The Secret to Results That Last

The end goal of habit change is to apply countless 1% improvements to enable your success. By themselves, these small changes will seem insignificant and futile because they are unlikely to make a difference. But as you stack them up, things begin to work to your advantage, and you will find it easier to maintain good habits.

Success is an ongoing process of fine-tuning; it is a system to help you improve. In Chapter 1, we established that failure to change or develop your habits is not your fault. The problem lies in the system for change.

The book has offered you a set of tools and strategies for developing better systems and forming better habits. These are condensed in the Four Laws of Behavior Change. You must make your habit evident so you will not forget it. If you do not feel like starting a habit, you must make it attractive, and if it becomes too difficult for you, make it easy. Make it satisfying, so you are motivated to stick to your habit.

However, if you are breaking a bad habit, you do the reverse of the Four Laws. You make the habit invisible, unattractive, challenging, and unsatisfying.

Habit formation and habit change are never-ending processes. Imagine what you can become if you do not stop improving yourself. And it all begins with a small habit.

That is the strength of atomic habits: small changes that lead to amazing results.

Little Lessons from the Four Laws

The book introduced you to a four-step framework for creating new habits: cue, craving, response, and reward. The model also bears remarkable insights into human behavior.

Awareness precedes desire. You notice a cue and assign a meaning to it. On the other hand, your brain defines your feelings and emotions to describe your current situation or environment. You cannot crave something unless you have noticed it.

Happiness is the absence of desire. Noticing a cue without craving for change indicates your contentment with your current situation. However, there will always be a new desire that comes along, so happiness is fleeting.

We form mental images of pleasure, and we are unsure what will happen when we attain that image because satisfaction is experienced after an action has happened.

When you do not desire to act on a cue that you observed, you realize that you do not need to fix anything. You experience peace.

If your craving and motivation are great enough, you will act on them no matter how difficult the situation may be.

Curiosity and motivation drive you to action that brings results; being smart does not compel you to action.

Emotions guide our behavior and influence our decisions. Craving comes before the response.

Our brain is programmed to feel; thinking is only secondary. This means we can only be rational and logical after we have been emotional.

Your response to a particular situation tends to go by your emotions. Two people may observe the same set of facts but respond differently because they process the facts through their unique emotional filter.

An appeal to emotion is more potent than an appeal to reason. Emotions are threats to wise decision-making.

Suffering propels progress. The desire to change is the source of all suffering and, ironically, progress. It is this desire that compels you to act. Craving makes you dissatisfied but driven; without craving, you are satisfied but lack ambition.

Your actions show how badly you want something; they reveal your true motivation

Response precedes the reward, which only comes after the energy is fully applied.

Self-control is not rewarding because it is not pleasurable. Resisting temptation ignores your craving.

The gap between our desire and our reward determines our level of satisfaction after an action has been performed. If the gap between expectations and outcomes is joy and delight, we are more likely to repeat the behavior. If it ends up in dissatisfaction or frustration, then there is only a slim chance of repetition.

If what you want exceeds what you like, you will be dissatisfied.

Happiness is relative.

The pain of failure is relative to the height of expectation.

Failure to attain something you want is more painful than failure to attain something you did not care about.

Feelings are experienced before and after the event. Before the event, you feel the craving that motivates you to act. After the event, you feel something that will make you want to repeat the action in the future.

Our feelings influence our actions, and our actions influence our feelings.

Desire and craving initiate a behavior. If the experience is not enjoyable, you are not compelled to repeat it. Satisfaction sustains your behavior.

Motivation gets you to act; succeeding gets you to repeat the action.

When we spot an opportunity for the first time, we hope to use it for what it could become. Our expectation is based only on what the opportunity promises. Next time, we have a more realistic expectation based on what transpired during the first time, and instead of hoping, we accept the likely outcomes.

Made in United States
North Haven, CT
11 January 2022

14597865R00071